This journal belongs to

_____

Date

_____

Thanks be to You, my Lord Jesus Christ,
for all the benefits You have given me,
for all the pains and insults
which You have borne for me.
O most merciful Redeemer, Friend, and Brother,
may I know You more clearly,
love You more dearly,
follow You more nearly,
day by day. Amen.

St. Richard of Chichester

This journal is filled with insights to help you see Jesus more clearly and practice coming into His presence anytime—morning, noon, or night. Jesus offers us interactive companionship so that we are never alone. He stands by our side ready to help us, guide us, and lead us into the life we were designed to experience.

With themes and quotes taken from my book *Practicing the Presence of Jesus*, this journal is a practical place to deepen your relationship with God's Son. Each section focuses on one way to come into the presence of Jesus. Find a safe place, pull up a chair, and visualize Jesus there sitting beside you— offering His love and friendship. Visualize Him speaking silently or aloud. It's not the technique that matters, but recognizing that He loves interacting with the real you and wants you to interact with the real Him.

Let this journal provide a place to write down how you have seen Jesus work in your life. Record reflections from your talks with God, dreams that Jesus has put in your heart, insights from Scripture, and any of the ways that you have come to know Jesus more fully. The goal is simple—the more your practice, the more you will truly see Jesus.

—Wally Armstrong

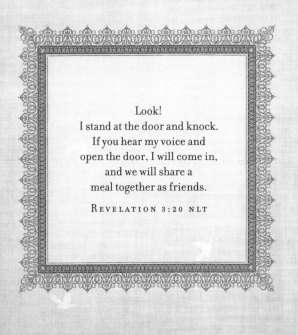

Look!
I stand at the door and knock.
If you hear my voice and
open the door, I will come in,
and we will share a
meal together as friends.

REVELATION 3:20 NLT

SEEING THE REAL JESUS

In Revelation there is a wonderful picture of Jesus standing at the door of our lives knocking. It says that if we will open our hearts and receive His presence, He will come in and transform our lives.

When Jesus was on earth and His disciples experienced His presence, they must have thought, "Now this is the way we were created to live. This is really living." It was transforming.

Now, as then, Jesus loves us unconditionally and gives us the freedom to choose every day whom we will follow and whether to invite Him in. Scripture says He is the same today as He was yesterday—meaning He will come in and change our lives if we will just open the door to Him. His presence is just as real now as it was then. He is ready to guide us into a life that is rich, abundant, and free.

God's desire is to have an intimate relationship with you. Take time each day to visualize Him walking shoulder to shoulder with you. Opening your heart to His presence is the first step.

The amazing truth is that Jesus is standing right beside each one of us,
offering us the life-changing gift of His friendship
and the promise of transformation from the inside out.

WALLY ARMSTRONG

Examine me, GOD...
Make sure I'm fit inside and out
So I never lose sight of your love,
But keep in step with you, never missing a beat.

PSALM 26:2–3 MSG

Nothing about our Lord Jesus Christ has changed down to this very hour.
His love has not changed. It hasn't cooled off, and it needs no increase
because He has already loved us with infinite love and there is no way
that infinitude can be increased.

A. W. TOZER

Jesus Christ is the same yesterday and today and forever.

HEBREWS 13:8 NIV

When we cry out with every fiber of our being, "My soul thirsts for God, for the living God," then, in time, there comes a seeing that is beyond sight. We begin to see a spiritual reality that others do not see. And we trust in that reality, betting our lives on it. This is what the Bible means by faith.

RICHARD J. FOSTER

Faith is the substance of things hoped for,
the evidence of things not seen.

HEBREWS 11:1 NKJV

The secret of our faith journey is found in seeing—
through the eyes of our heart—the presence of our unseen Friend.

MARTIN LUTHER

Though you have not seen him, you love him; and even though you do not see him now,
you believe in him and are filled with an inexpressible and glorious joy,
for you are receiving the end result of your faith, the salvation of your souls.

1 PETER 1:8–9 NIV

You need not cry very loud; He is nearer to us than we think.

BROTHER LAWRENCE

Evening and morning and at noon
I will pray, and cry aloud,
And He shall hear my voice.

PSALM 55:17 NKJV

God may be invisible, but He's in touch. You may not be able to see Him,
but He is in control. And that includes you—your circumstances.
That includes what you've just lost. That includes what you've just gained.
That includes all of life—past, present, future.

CHARLES R. SWINDOLL

We fix our eyes not on what is seen, but on what is unseen,
since what is seen is temporary, but what is unseen is eternal.

2 CORINTHIANS 4:18 NIV

I am both with you and within you. I go before you
to open up the way, and I also walk alongside you.
There could never be another companion as devoted as I am.

SARAH YOUNG

How great is the goodness
you have stored up for those who fear you....
You hide them in the shelter of your presence.

PSALM 31:19—20 NLT

If we really believe not only that God exists but also that
He is actively present in our lives—healing, teaching, guiding—
we need to set aside a time and space to give Him our undivided attention.

HENRI J. M. NOUWEN

God is our refuge and strength, an ever-present help in trouble.
Therefore we will not fear.... The LORD Almighty is with us.

PSALM 46:1–2, 7 NIV

This is and has been the Father's work from the beginning—
to bring us into the home of His heart.

GEORGE MACDONALD

I pray that Christ will be more and more at home in your hearts,
living within you as you trust in him.

EPHESIANS 3:17 TLB

If anyone is in Christ,
the new creation has come:
the old has gone,
the new is here!

2 CORINTHIANS 5:17 NIV

seeing yourself as jesus sees you

The Bible tells us that when we believe in Jesus and place our trust in Him, we become new creations, whole new persons. This may be hard to believe but it's true—simply because our loving and merciful God, the creator of all reality, has decided to make it so.

You couldn't be loved more than you are at this very moment, because you are loved with the same perfect love that the Father has for His Son. This is a gift that is given freely.

By believing in Jesus, you become a totally new person. He loves you just for who you are, as you are—no strings attached. He sees you as valuable, lovable, as His friend. That is how He wants you to see yourself. But that way of looking at yourself takes a little practice.

We only know ourselves as God searches us. "God knows me" is different from "God is omniscient." The latter is a mere theological statement; the former is a child of God's most precious possession.

Oswald Chambers

O LORD, You have searched me and known me.

PSALM 139:1 NKJV

God created you for a purpose. He absolutely adores you.
He will have his love lived out through you. For this we were made.

BILL THRALL, BRUCE McNICOL, AND JOHN S. LYNCH

God wanted them to look for him and perhaps search all around for him and find him, though he is not far from any of us: "By his power we live and move and exist."

ACTS 17:27—28 NCV

When we are away from God, He misses us far more than we miss Him.

RUTH BELL GRAHAM

I've called your name. You're mine.
When you're in over your head, I'll be there with you....
Because I am GOD, your personal God.

ISAIAH 43:1–3 MSG

Nothing we can do will make the Father love us less; nothing we do can make Him love us more. He loves us unconditionally with an everlasting love. All He asks of us is that we respond to Him with the free will that He has given to us.

NANCIE CARMICHAEL

If God gives such attention to the appearance of wildflowers—
most of which are never even seen—don't you think he'll attend to you,
take pride in you, do his best for you?

MATTHEW 6:30–31 MSG

You can talk to God because God listens. Your voice matters in heaven. He takes you very seriously. When you enter His presence, the attendants turn to you to hear your voice. No need to fear that you will be ignored. Even if you stammer or stumble, even if what you have to say impresses no one, it impresses God—and He listens.

MAX LUCADO

"Then you will call on me and come and pray to me, and I will listen to you.
You will seek me and find me when you seek me with all your heart.
I will be found by you," declares the LORD.

JEREMIAH 29:12—14 NIV

God not only knows us, but He values us highly in spite of all He knows....
You and I are the creatures He prizes above the rest of His creation. We are made
in His image, and He sacrificed His Son that each one of us might be one with Him.

JOHN FISHER

Are not five sparrows sold for two pennies? Yet not one of them
is forgotten by God. Indeed, the very hairs of your head are all numbered.
Don't be afraid; you are worth more than many sparrows.

LUKE 12:6–7 NIV

He [God] knows everything about us. And He cares about everything.
Moreover, He can manage every situation. And He loves us! Surely this is enough
to open the wellsprings of joy…. And joy is always a source of strength.

Hannah Whitall Smith

The LORD is my strength and shield.
I trust him, and he helps me.
I am very happy,
and I praise him with my song.

PSALM 28:7 NCV

God loves you more than you'll ever know. Not your image, not your happy face, not your spirituality—but you. The real you. The one you think nobody knows about. No, real love is *not* blind. Because His eyes are always open, He can see what you cannot. And He felt what He saw in you was worth dying for.

BINGHAM HUNTER

Your *real* life…is with Christ in God. *He* is your life.

COLOSSIANS 3:3 MSG

I'm no longer calling you
servants because servants don't
understand what their master
is thinking and planning. No,
I've named you friends because
I've let you in on everything I've
heard from the Father.

JOHN 15:15 MSG

Seeing Jesus as Your Friend

When Jesus called the disciples to follow Him, it was His life they were drawn to. His personality. He offered them friendship. It wasn't about the prestige, the travel, or the book deals. It was about a relationship.

Jesus offers us the same companionship He offered the disciples. He still speaks. His Words still comfort. His Presence is still available to us right where we are.

The depth of the relationship is up to you. Just like any good friend, Jesus wants to be invited into every area of your life. Open your heart and let Him in.

Jesus said that He tells His friends all that His Father has told Him;
close friends communicate thoroughly and make a transfer of heart and thought.
How awesome is our opportunity to be friends with God, the almighty Creator of all!

BEVERLY LAHAYE

We can rejoice in our wonderful new relationship with God
because our Lord Jesus Christ has made us friends of God.

ROMANS 5:11 NLT

The disciples knew what it was like to be Jesus' friend,
and it was this dynamic friendship with Him
that made all the difference in their lives.

WALLY ARMSTRONG

Some friends play at friendship but a true friend
sticks closer than one's nearest kin.

PROVERBS 18:24 NRSV

Knowing what to say is not always necessary;
just the presence of a caring friend can make a world of difference.

Sheri Curry

You will show me the path of life;
In Your presence is fullness of joy;
At Your right hand are pleasures forevermore.

PSALM 16:11 NKJV

I drove away from my mind everything capable of spoiling the sense of the presence of God.... My soul has had a habitual, silent, secret conversation with God.

BROTHER LAWRENCE

Find a quiet, secluded place so you won't be tempted to role-play before God.
Just be there as simply and honestly as you can manage.
The focus will shift from you to God, and you will begin to sense his grace.

MATTHEW 6:6 MSG

Jesus wants to be more than my best Friend.
He also wants me to enter a partnership with Him.

LANA KROFFT

This is the secret: Christ lives in you. This gives you assurance of sharing his glory.

COLOSSIANS 1:27 NLT

A rule I have had for years is: to treat the Lord Jesus Christ as a personal friend.
His is not a creed, a mere empty doctrine, but it is He Himself we have.

DWIGHT L. MOODY.

Steep yourself in God-reality, God-initiative, God-provisions.
You'll find all your everyday human concerns will be met.
Don't be afraid of missing out. You're my dearest friends!

LUKE 12:30—31 MSG

The Christian faith is meant to be lived moment by moment.
It isn't some broad, general outline—it's a long walk with a real Person.

JONI EARECKSON TADA

Blessed are those who have learned to acclaim you,
who walk in the light of your presence, LORD.

PSALM 89:15 NIV

_____

_____

_____

_____

_____

_____

_____

_____

_____

_____

_____

_____

_____

_____

_____

_____

_____

_____

_____

> True friendship with God...means being so intimately in touch with God
> that you never even need to ask Him to show you His will.
> You are God's will. And all of your seemingly commonsense decisions
> are actually His will for you, unless you sense a check in your spirit.
>
> OSWALD CHAMBERS

We continually ask God to fill you with the knowledge of his will through all the wisdom and understanding that the Spirit gives.

COLOSSIANS 1:9 NIV

Who you are with is who you will be like.

WALLY ARMSTRONG

Dear friends, now we are children of God, and what we will be has not yet been
made known. But we know that when Christ appears, we shall be like him.

1 JOHN 3:2 NIV

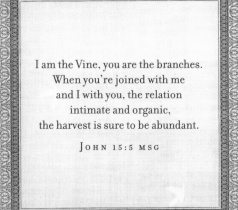

I am the Vine, you are the branches.
When you're joined with me
and I with you, the relation
intimate and organic,
the harvest is sure to be abundant.

JOHN 15:5 MSG

SEEING YOURSELF
AS AN EXTENSION OF JESUS

Jesus shares the secret of being connected to Him by drawing a beautiful picture in which He is the vine and we are the branches. We draw our nourishment through our companionship with Him. We become an extension of His strength, His sheltering love, His grace. This becomes our way of life.

As our friendship with Jesus grows, we see wonderful fruits of the Spirit bloom and grow within us. We find ourselves allowing His love to flow through us. We are energized through His friendship, and because of it we begin to look and act like Him.

Take time to think about the ways you are an extension of His love. As you connect with Him, His life flows through you to connect with others. As you are fed, they are fed, and you become an extension of Jesus.

Dear Lord,...shine through me, and be so in me that every soul
I come in contact with may feel Your presence in my soul....
Let me thus praise You in the way You love best, by shining on those around me.

JOHN HENRY NEWMAN

Don't hide your light! Let it shine for all; let your good deeds glow
for all to see, so that they will praise your heavenly Father.

MATTHEW 5:16 TLB

"Blessed are those who hunger and thirst after righteousness."
This beatitude reflects true spiritual passion, an insatiable hunger
to know God intimately, to model His ways personally.

CHARLES R. SWINDOLL

Live a life worthy of the Lord and please him in every way:
bearing fruit in every good work, growing in the knowledge of God.

COLOSSIANS 1:10 NIV

It is not the great deeds but the small ones that usher in the kingdom
of heaven most powerfully. When one is perfectly content to have
a life that is small and ordinary, then one's life becomes great.

MIKE MASON

Everything else is worthless when compared with the infinite value
of knowing Christ Jesus my Lord.

PHILIPPIANS 3:8 NLT

Everyone has inside himself a piece of good news! The good news is that
you really don't know how great you can be, how much you can love,
what you can accomplish and what your potential is.

ANNE FRANK

Why is it that he gives us these special abilities to do certain things best?
It is that God's people will be equipped to do better work for him.

EPHESIANS 4:12 TLB

As you live in close contact with Me, the light of my presence
filters through you to bless others.

SARAH YOUNG

May God be gracious to us and bless us and make his face shine upon us,
that your ways may be known on earth, your salvation among all nations.

PSALM 67:1–2 NIV

I am blessed. I can bless. So this is happiness....
I am a flame to light other flames.

A N N   V O S K A M P

It is the God who commanded light to shine out of darkness,
who has shone in our hearts.

2 CORINTHIANS 4:6 NKJV

Truly charity has no limit; for the love of God has been poured into our hearts…
inviting us to bloom in the garden where He has planted.

St. Francis de Sales

The one who plants and the one who waters work together with the same purpose. And both will be rewarded for their own hard work. For we are both God's workers.

1 CORINTHIANS 3:8—9 NLT

What think we of Christ? Is He altogether glorious in our eyes,
and precious to our hearts? May Christ be our joy, our confidence, our all.
May we daily be made more like Him, and more devoted to His service.

MATTHEW HENRY

As for me and my house, we will serve the LORD.

JOSHUA 24:15 NKJV

You are not here in the world for yourself. You have been
sent here for others. The world is waiting for you!

Live out your God-created identity. Live generously
and graciously toward others, the way God lives toward you.

MATTHEW 5:48 MSG

I cry to you for help, LORD;
in the morning my prayer
comes before you.

PSALM 88:13 NIV

STARTING YOUR DAY WITH JESUS

Jesus' life is the perfect model for us. He had an ongoing conversation with His Father no matter where He was. Yet, He also took time to slip away to be alone with God to refresh and plan. He rose early to have prayer time. He was in constant companionship with God. Nothing was more important.

When we start our day with God, we are more likely to have an interactive conversation with Him throughout the day. We find ourselves becoming closer and closer friends. By spending quiet time in prayer, we become more and more like Jesus.

Start each morning in prayer and you'll feel His presence all day long. Try writing down your prayers. Record requests, prayers that are answered, or the prayers from the Bible that touch your heart in a special way. Prayer journaling is another way to have a conversation with Jesus.

I have been away and come back again many times to this place.
Each time I approach, I regret ever having left. There is a peace here,
a serenity, even before I enter. Just the idea of returning becomes
a balm for the wounds I've collected elsewhere. Before I can finish
even one knock, the door opens wide and I am in His presence.

BARBARA FARMER

I pray that God, the source of hope, will fill you completely
with joy and peace because you trust in him. Then you will overflow
with confident hope through the power of the Holy Spirit.

ROMANS 15:13 NLT

Prayer can only be appreciated when you actually spend time in it.
Spending time with the Master will elevate your thinking.
The more you pray, the more will be revealed. You will appreciate
not only the greatness of prayer, but the greatness of God.

JONI EARECKSON TADA

Give attention to your servant's prayer and his plea for mercy, LORD my God.
Hear the cry and the prayer that your servant is praying in your presence this day.

1 KINGS 8:28 NIV

Your walk with God is essential. His heart is not seen in an occasional chat or weekly visit. We learn His will as we take up residence in His house every single day.

MAX LUCADO

I love the Lord because he hears my prayers and answers them.
Because he bends down and listens, I will pray as long as I breathe!

PSALM 116:1—2 TLB

He does want to speak to us—to you—today. In your own language,
just as a friend would speak. We simply need to take the time to listen.

WALLY ARMSTRONG

Listen to me…you whom I have upheld since your birth,
and have carried since you were born. Even to your old age and gray hairs I am he,
I am he who will sustain you. I have made you and I will carry you.

ISAIAH 46:3–4 NIV

Let the Light of My Presence soak into you, as you focus your thoughts on Me....
Do not skimp on our time together. Resist the clamor of tasks waiting to be done.
You have chosen what is better, and it will not be taken away from you.

SARAH YOUNG

I ask—ask the God of our Master, Jesus Christ, the God of glory—to make you intelligent and discerning in knowing him personally, your eyes focused and clear, so that you can see exactly what it is he is calling you to do.

EPHESIANS 1:17–19 MSG

The end of prayer is that I come to know God Himself.

O S W A L D C H A M B E R S

Let us look only to Jesus, the One who began our faith and who makes it perfect.

HEBREWS 12:2 NCV

Without the concrete and specific involvement of daily life we cannot come
to know the loving presence of Him who holds us in the palm of His hand....
Therefore, we are called each day to present to our Lord the whole of our lives.

HENRI J. M. NOUWEN

Take your everyday, ordinary life—your sleeping, eating, going-to-work, and walking-around life—and place it before God as an offering. Embracing what God does for you is the best thing you can do for him.

ROMANS 12:1 MSG

So wait before the Lord. Wait in the stillness. And in that stillness, assurance will come to you. You will know that you are heard; you will know that your Lord ponders the voice of your humble desires; you will hear quiet words spoken to you yourself, perhaps to your grateful surprise and refreshment.

AMY CARMICHAEL

Be still, and know that I am God.

PSALM 46:10 NIV

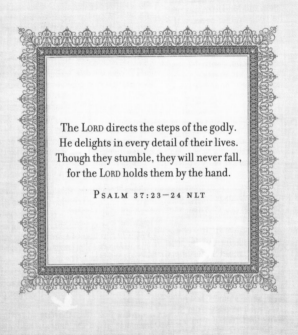

The LORD directs the steps of the godly.
He delights in every detail of their lives.
Though they stumble, they will never fall,
for the LORD holds them by the hand.

PSALM 37:23—24 NLT

SEEING JESUS AS YOUR GUIDE

J esus calls to us with His simple invitation to follow Him from right where we are. He asks us to trust Him and to learn from Him. He has a plan for each life. We discover His plan for us by reading His Word, through the wisdom of others, and in our conversations with Him. Through it all, He guides us. Sometimes the plan is laid out in front of us and other times we only see the first step.

As you journal you will begin to see how Jesus has guided you. Through your joys, struggles, and experiences He has been there with you. And He always will be. He lovingly assures you that all is well and that He is with you no matter what the world throws your way.

Living your life hand in hand, shoulder to shoulder with Jesus and recording that journey will enable your trust in Him to grow and your steps to become surer. Just keep following your friend and guide.

God's wisdom is always available to help us choose from
alternatives we face, and help us to follow His eternal plan for us.

Gloria Gaither

Commit to the LORD whatever you do,
and he will establish your plans.

PROVERBS 16:3 NIV

When you come to the end of all the light you know, and it's time to step into
the darkness of the unknown, faith is knowing that one of two things shall happen:
Either you will be given something solid to stand on or you will be taught to fly.

EDWARD TELLER

For we walk by faith, not by sight.

2 CORINTHIANS 5:7 NKJV

Incredible as it may seem, God wants our companionship.
He wants to have us close to Him. He wants to be a father to us, to shield us,
to protect us, to counsel us, and to guide us in our way through life.

BILLY GRAHAM

So do not fear, for I am with you; do not be dismayed, for I am your God.
I will strengthen you and help you; I will uphold you with my righteous right hand.

ISAIAH 41:10 NIV

God has designs on our future...and He has designed us for the future.
He has given us something to do in the future that no one else can do.

RUTH SENTER

I have it all planned out—plans to take care of you, not abandon you,
plans to give you the future you hope for.

JEREMIAH 29:11 MSG

Faith is not intellectual understanding; faith is a deliberate commitment
to the person of Jesus Christ, even when I can't see the way ahead.

OSWALD CHAMBERS

The gatekeeper opens the gate for him, and the sheep listen
to his voice. He calls his own sheep by name and leads them out.
When he has brought out all his own, he goes on ahead of them,
and his sheep follow him because they know his voice.

JOHN 10:3–4 NIV

Practice His presence by simply keeping Jesus in sight.
It is really the process of seeing every situation through His eyes,
making sure to act and react in a way that follows His lead.

WALLY ARMSTRONG

I will lead the blind by ways they have not known,
along unfamiliar paths I will guide them; I will turn the darkness
into light before them and make the rough places smooth.

ISAIAH 42:16 NIV

Heaven often seems distant and unknown,
but if He who made the road…is our guide, we need not fear to lose the way.

HENRY VAN DYKE

This God is our God for ever and ever;
he will be our guide even to the end.

PSALM 48:14 NIV

Know by the light of faith that God is present,
and be content with directing all your actions toward Him.

BROTHER LAWRENCE

In everything you do, put God first, and he will direct you
and crown your efforts with success.

PROVERBS 3:6 TLB

God's hand is always there;
once you grasp it you'll never want to let it go.

I am always with you;
you hold me by my right hand.

PSALM 73:23 NIV

Surely I am with you always,
to the very end of the age.

MATTHEW 28:20 NIV

SEEING JESUS
AS AN ALL-DAY COMPANION

Jesus loves being a part of our lives every minute of each day, no matter what is going on at that moment. When the world comes flying at us with temptations and worries, He loves helping us with those. Throughout the day He stands ready to be consulted and to guide us into His presence. Jesus goes with us and wants to be involved not only during the difficult times but also as we celebrate the simple joys.

It's important to visualize Jesus by our side all day, every day. With His nearness, we have the wisdom and power to make good choices. The more we seek to listen to His still small voice, the more we will experience His presence.

Even though the presence of Jesus is not visible, it is just as accessible and real as the ground you stand on. As you seek His unseen presence, you will discover that your Friend Jesus is available to you in every moment.

Always be in a state of expectancy, and see that you leave room for God to come in as He likes.

OSWALD CHAMBERS

The LORD is good to those who wait for Him,
To the soul who seeks Him.
It is good that one should hope and wait quietly
For the salvation of the Lord.

LAMENTATIONS 3:25—26 NKJV

We are not alone on our journey. The God of love who gave us life sent us [His] only
Son to be with us at all times and in all places, so that we never have to feel lost in
our struggles but always can trust that God walks with us.

HENRI J. M. NOUWEN

Let your unfailing love surround us, LORD, for our hope is in you alone.

PSALM 33:22 NLT

Life in the presence of God should be known to us in conscious experience.
It is a life to be enjoyed every moment of every day.

A. W. Tozer

We throw open our doors to God and discover at the same moment
that he has already thrown open his door to us. We find ourselves standing
where we always hoped we might stand—out in the wide open spaces
of God's grace and glory, standing tall and shouting our praise.

ROMANS 5:2 MSG

The Lord's goodness surrounds us at every moment.
I walk through it almost with difficulty, as through thick grass and flowers.

R. W. Barber

Trust in him at all times…pour out your hearts to him, for God is our refuge.

PSALM 62:8 NIV

God is every moment totally aware of each one of us.
Totally aware in intense concentration and love.... No one passes through
any area of life, happy or tragic, without the attention of God with them.

EUGENIA PRICE

Keep me as the apple of your eye; hide me in the shadow of your wings.

PSALM 17:8 NIV

Nothing can separate you from [God's] love, absolutely nothing....
God is enough for time, and God is enough for eternity. God is enough!

HANNAH WHITALL SMITH

I am convinced that neither death nor life, neither angels nor demons,
neither the present nor the future, nor any powers, neither height nor depth,
nor anything else in all creation, will be able to separate us from
the love of God that is in Christ Jesus our Lord.

ROMANS 8:38—39 NIV

There isn't a certain time we should set aside to talk about God.
God is part of our every waking moment.

Marva Collins

GOD promises to love me all day,
sing songs all through the night! My life is God's prayer.

PSALM 42:8 MSG

God does not promise to bail us out of every uncomfortable situation.
But He does assure us that He will be with us throughout our difficult times.
His presence makes all the difference.

GOD said, "My presence will go with you. I'll see the journey to the end."

EXODUS 33:14 MSG

We are always in the presence of God.... There is never a non-sacred moment!
His presence never diminishes. Our awareness of His presence may falter,
but the reality of His presence never changes.

MAX LUCADO

Now we can come fearlessly right into God's presence,
assured of his glad welcome when we come with Christ and trust in him.

EPHESIANS 3:12 TLB

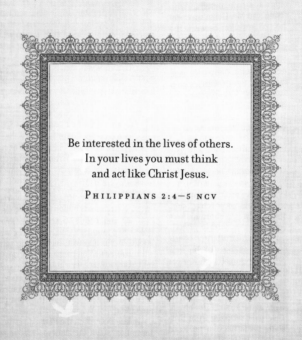

Be interested in the lives of others.
In your lives you must think
and act like Christ Jesus.

PHILIPPIANS 2:4–5 NCV

SEEING OTHERS AS JESUS SEES THEM

Jesus calls us to be light in the world. Since we become like those with whom we rub elbows, we will become more Christlike the closer we get to Him. When we're friends with Him, He will bring people across our path for us to love with genuine love. And as we walk together with them, we will be able to share His love.

Every person has a story to tell. We all want to be known and loved. But it can be scary to trust others with our story. When our friendships center on Jesus, His presence removes that fear. He builds and strengthens our relationships. He encourages our hearts to see others as He sees them. Valuable. Beautiful. Love-worthy.

As your own friendship with Jesus deepens, you will naturally begin loving others.

If there has come to us the miracle of friendship, if there is a soul
to which our soul has been drawn, it is surely worthwhile being loyal and true.

HUGH BLACK

If you love someone, you will be loyal to him no matter what the cost.
You will always believe in him, always expect the best of him,
and always stand your ground in defending him.

1 Corinthians 13:7 tlb

To be in the image of God means that all of us are made for the purpose of knowing and loving God and one another and of being loved in turn.

ROBERTA BONDI

Let love and faithfulness never leave you; bind them around your neck,
write them on the tablet of your heart.

PROVERBS 3:3 NIV

It doesn't take a huge spotlight to draw attention to how great our God is.
All it takes is for one committed person to so let his light shine before
men that a world lost in darkness welcomes the light.

GARY SMALLEY AND JOHN TRENT

May God be gracious to us and bless us and make his face shine upon us,
that your ways may be known on earth, your salvation among all nations.

PSALM 67:1–2 NIV

Whatever the circumstances, whatever the call,
whatever the duty, whatever the price, whatever the sacrifice—
God's strength will be your strength in your hour of need.

BILLY GRAHAM

Look to the LORD and his strength;
seek his face always.

PSALM 105:4 NIV

If we truly love people, we will desire for them far more
than that which is within our power to give them,
and this will lead us to prayer. Intercession is a way of loving others.

RICHARD J. FOSTER

I urge you, first of all, to pray for all people. Ask God to help them;
intercede on their behalf, and give thanks for them.

1 TIMOTHY 2:1 NLT

Our sweetest experiences of affection are meant to point us
to that realm which is the real and endless home of the heart.

HENRY WARD BEECHER

What happens when we live God's way? He brings gifts into our lives,
much the same way that fruit appears in an orchard—things like affection
for others, exuberance about life, serenity.

GALATIANS 5:22 MSG

It is through the living witness of others that we are drawn to God at all.
It is because of His creatures, and His work in them, that we come to praise Him.

TERESA OF AVILA

I will tell of the kindnesses of the LORD, the deeds for which he is to be praised, according to all the LORD has done for us—yes, the many good things he has done... according to his compassion and many kindnesses.

ISAIAH 63:7 NIV

Dear Lord…
Stay with us and then we shall begin to shine as You shine….
It will be You shining on others through us.

MOTHER TERESA

Go into all the world and preach the gospel to all creation.

MARK 16:15 NIV

Our goal is sharing and showing love within the community where God has placed us and inviting others into the incredible friendship that Jesus offers.

WALLY ARMSTRONG

Love one another the way I loved you. This is the very best way to love.
Put your life on the line for your friends.

JOHN 15:12–13 MSG

Ellie Claire® Gift & Paper Corp.
Brentwood, TN 37027
EllieClaire.com

Practicing the Presence of Jesus Journal
© 2013 by Ellie Claire Gift & Paper Corp.
ISBN 978-1-60936-590-5

Scripture references are from the following sources: The Holy Bible, New International Version®
NIV®. © 1973, 1978, 1984, 2011 by Biblica, Inc.™. Used by permission of Zondervan. All rights
reserved worldwide. *The Message* (MSG). Copyright © 1993, 1994, 1995, 1996, 2000, 2001, 2002
by Eugene Peterson. Used by permission of NavPress, Colorado Springs, CO. The Holy Bible, New
Living Translation (NLT). Copyright © 1996, 2004, 2007 by Tyndale House Foundation. Used
by permission of Tyndale House Publishers, Inc., Carol Stream, Illinois 60188. The New Revised
Standard Version Bible (NRSV), copyright 1989, 1995, Division of Christian Education of the
National Council of the Churches of Christ in the United States of America. Used by permission.
The Living Bible (TLB) © 1971. Used by permission of Tyndale House Publishers, Inc., Carol
Stream, Illinois 60188. The New Century Version˚ (NCV). Copyright © 1987, 1988, 1991, 2005
by Thomas Nelson, Inc. Used by permission. The Holy Bible, New King James Version (NKJV).
Copyright © 1982 by Thomas Nelson, Inc. Used by permission. All rights reserved.

Excluding Scripture verses and deity pronouns, in some quotations references to men and
masculine pronouns have been replaced with gender-neutral or feminine references. Additionally,
in some quotations we have carefully updated wording that may distract modern readers.

Compiled by Marilyn Jansen
Cover and interior design by Gearbox | studiogearbox.com

Ellie Claire Gift & Paper Corp. is an imprint of Worthy Publishing.

Printed in China